Let's Go FISHING

FOREWORD BY
MIKE IACONELLI

JOSHUA MUTTERS
GABBY CORREIA

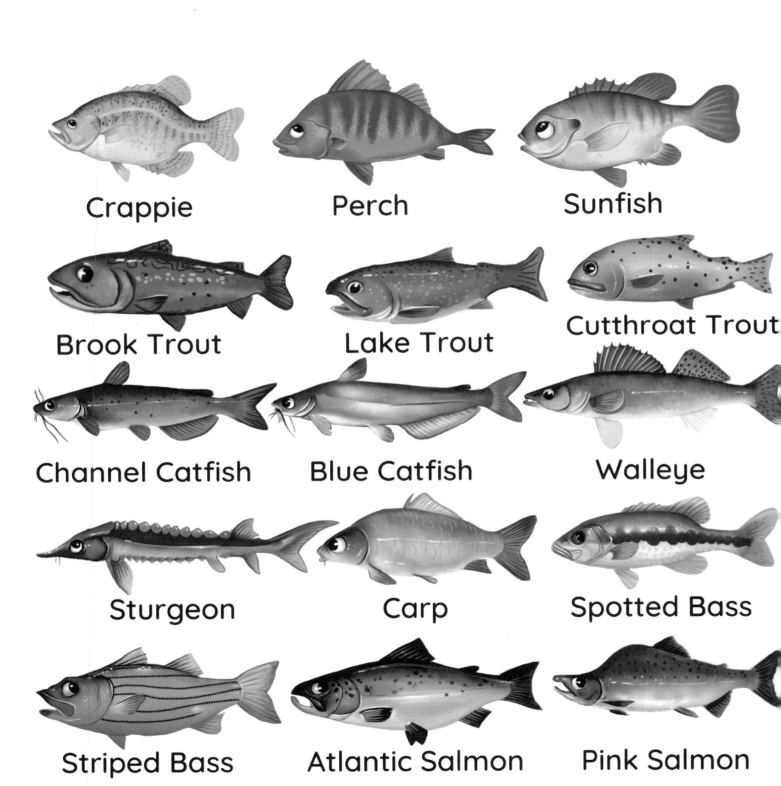

Crappie

Perch

Sunfish

Brook Trout

Lake Trout

Cutthroat Trout

Channel Catfish

Blue Catfish

Walleye

Sturgeon

Carp

Spotted Bass

Striped Bass

Atlantic Salmon

Pink Salmon

Bluegill

Pike

Brown Trout

Musky

Rainbow Trout

Flathead Catfish

Smallmouth Bass

Largemouth Bass

Coho Salmon

Chinook Salmon

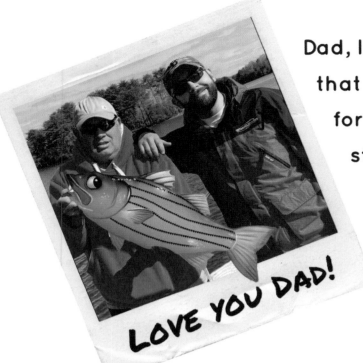

Dad, I am so grateful for the example
that you set as a father. Thank you
for always working so hard and
still taking the time to foster
my passion for the outdoors.

LOVE YOU DAD!

Joshua Mutters, Author

Gabriella Correia, Illustrator

Grander
>>>> PUBLISHING →

LET'S GO FISHING

"Let's Go Fishing is a wonderful book that makes it fun for kids to learn about all the freshwater fish species and introduces them to fishing and being in the outdoors. I'm really excited to be a part of it!"

- Mike Iaconelli

Let's go
fishing together,
yes fishing is fun.

It might be
the greatest thing
under the sun.

The first things that you need are a rod and a reel.

Bring line, baits, and hooks, with some patience and skill.

You can fish from a bank, kayak, boat, or canoe in lakes, rivers, streams, and in ponds or creeks, too.

We will stick with just freshwater, no salt you see.
There are plenty of fish there for you and for me.

There are many panfish, like crappie and perch.

Finding sunfish and bluegill is worth a quick search.

You can also catch trout
such as rainbow

All catfish have whiskers,
I promise it's true.

There are flathead, and channel,
and some that are blue.

Watch for teeth in the musky,
the walleye, and pike.

Oh, reeling them in
is such fun
if you get them
to strike.

The sturgeon and carp
both grow big near the bottom.

To catch them add sinkers,
that is if you've got them.

That brings us to bass.
There are largemouth and small,
some spotted, some striped,
I just love catching all!

There's salmon:
Atlantic, pinks, coho, chinook.

Just how many fish
can we fit in this book?

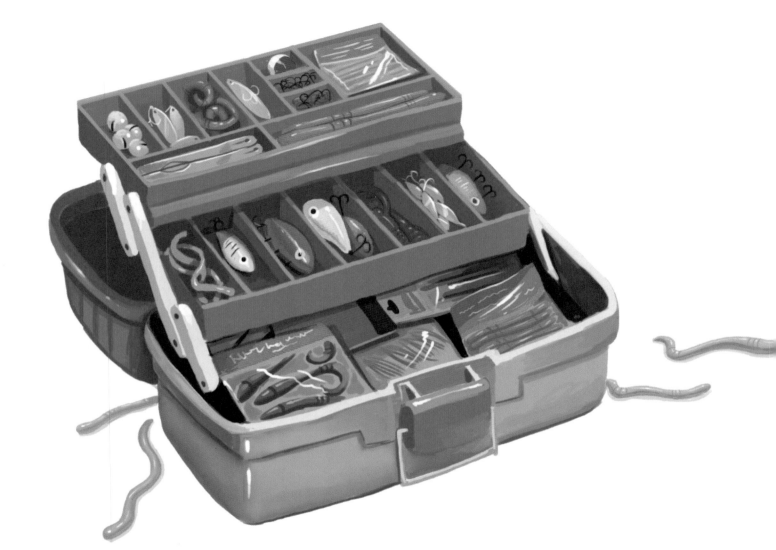

We now know all fish
that there are and that's great!
Let's focus on lures
and the types of each bait.

Some anglers use live bait
like minnows or worms,
a crawfish, a shad, or a lizard that squirms.

Yet, others use fake flies to lure in their catch.

They use what looks real,
so it matches the
hatch.

Many anglers
love baits
that are made
from soft plastic.
They catch
lots of fish
and that's
pretty fantastic.

The lures move through water from bottom to top.

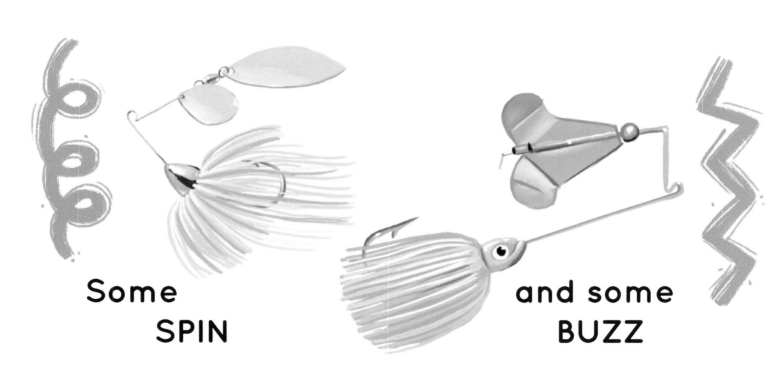

Some
SPIN

and some
BUZZ

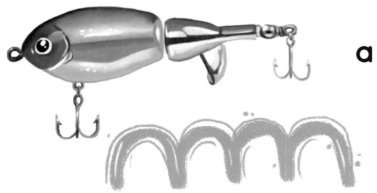

and some
plop, PLOP,
plop, PLOP.

You may fish
by yourself

with a friend
or with two

Junior Angler Club

Luxley Mutters	Elliana Hager
Zeke Mutters	Caden Berry
Paisley Morgan	Cohen Caldwell
Arrow Morgan	Madison Slone
Baustin Morgan	Brodie O'Malley
Charlotte Flint	Kalyn Diegert
Maggie Flint	Miles Young
Lila Jean Solze	Leslie Williamson
Elijah Harris	Kinley Street
RJ Speaks	Mason Spolarich
Theodore James Thompson	Kayden Spolarich
Sophia Grace Thompson	Santino Michael DeCrosta
Rodes Shearer Chen-Ludwig	Gracelyn Griggs
Christian McFarland	Luke Overstreet
Matthew McFarland	Dillon Darrington
Ceci Newman	DJ Darrington
Jack Newman	Miles Darrington
John B. Riley	Tristin Simmons
Sophia Rose Garcia	Harper Briskie
Owen Newton	Noah Briones
Cohl Newton	Chloe Briones
Jase Newton	Vegas Iaconelli
Luke Newton	Estella Iaconelli
Carson Taylor Dunn	Daniel Griscom
Luca Lee	Maddox Green
Julian DeWitt	Luke Lepp
Korrigan Ward	Amias Sanders
MacIntyre Ward	

Sponsors

theikefoundation.org

The Ike Foundation® is a non-profit organization founded by Mike and Becky Iaconelli. Their mission is to introduce urban and rural children to the wholesome sport of fishing while instilling in them a love and respect for the outdoors.

kkhomes.com

aftco.com

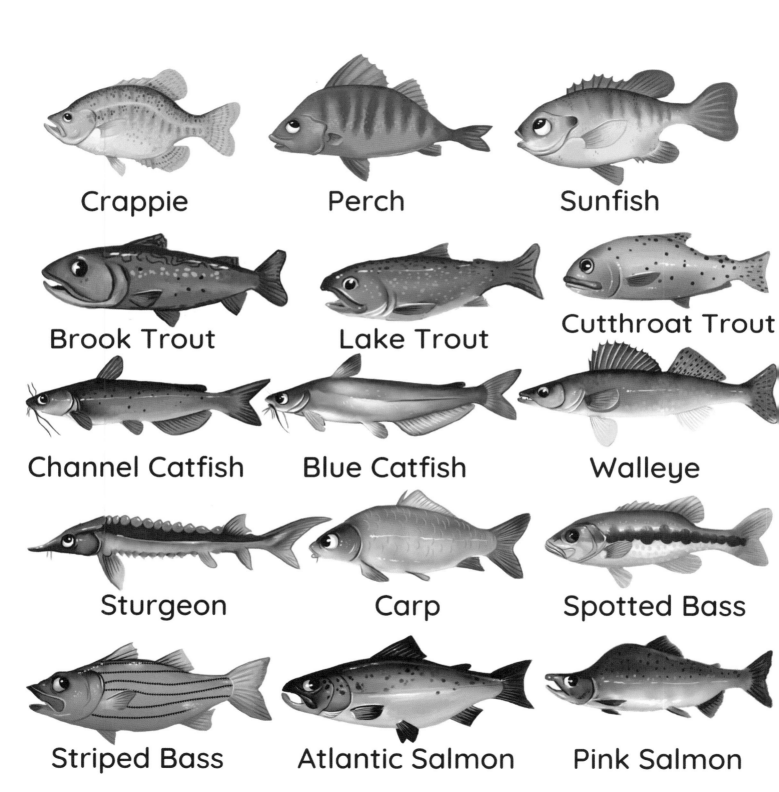

Crappie

Perch

Sunfish

Brook Trout

Lake Trout

Cutthroat Trout

Channel Catfish

Blue Catfish

Walleye

Sturgeon

Carp

Spotted Bass

Striped Bass

Atlantic Salmon

Pink Salmon

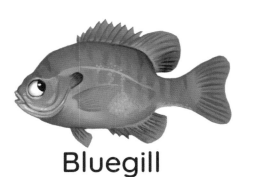

Bluegill

Pike

Brown Trout

Musky

Rainbow Trout

Flathead Catfish

Smallmouth Bass

Largemouth Bass

Coho Salmon

Chinook Salmon

Printed in Great Britain
by Amazon

ARTIST - ILLUSTRATOR - AUTHOR
www.nonaGallery.com

@nonaGalleryArt

Table
of
Contents

- INTRODUCTION -

Welcome To The World Of The Horoscope Witches!

Where do the Horoscopes come from? The Horoscopes come from a circular band in the sky called the Zodiac, which extends about eight degrees on either side of the apparent path of the sun through the sky, also known as the ecliptic. Within the Zodiac there are twelve houses.

It is believed that it was the ancient Babylonians who first divided the Zodiac into twelve, using major constellations found within each section to name each house. However, the signs as we know them today no longer correspond with the constellations, as three thousand years have passed and the Earth's axis has a slight wobble to it. This means that the zones of the Zodiac as we see them from Earth are no longer in line with the constellations that give them their names. According to astrologers everybody's characteristics and personality can be determined by the sign of the zodiac and its ruling heavenly body paramount at their birth. A person's horoscope from just their zodiac house is actually of little value and not particularly accurate, exactitude in both time of birth and also the position of the heavenly bodies is essential, as each has an effect upon the other. The houses of the zodiac are also divided into three groups, cardinal, fixed, and mutable, and then these three are then divided again into the four elements of fire, earth, air, and water. All these aspects have to be considered when creating a horoscope.

Almost all of us know our horoscope sign, these signs are supposedly a portrait of character and abilities and, for some, can be remarkably accurate if you are what is deemed as a "pure zodiac type". This is someone whose horoscope is heavily influenced by one particular sign. If however from your horoscope you are able to recognise some aspects of your character, but not all, this could be for many reasons but if you were born near the start or end of a Zodiac house you may have traits for the sign that was before or after your own as well. Using these Zodiac houses I have created twelve Horoscope Witches that have appropriately matched magical powers and personalities. As well as each having a familiar. A familiar isn't just a pet or companion to a witch, it is, in fact, part of them, and if any harm befell a familiar, the witch themselves would be affected too.

Lucy I hope
you like the
book! :)
Nona xx.

FINE ART PRINTS

Stickers &
Stationary

MAGICAL BOOKS

All Direct From The Artist

@nonaGalleryArt

TALISMAN
ENAMEL PIN
COLLECTION

Familiars
Handmade Necklace Collection

KEYRINGS &
ACCESSORIES

All Direct From The Artist
www.nonaGallery.com

- The Horoscope Witches -

I hope you enjoy the information I have gathered and the characters I have designed, and I especially hope you like, and can relate to, the Horoscope Witch that is for your own zodiac sign.

- ARIES -
The Blood Witch
March 21 - April 20

|

Brazen and passionate, their driven attitude makes them excellent coven leaders. Preferring to use more tangible spells, they always use brute force when spell casting.

- ARIES -
The Blood Witch

The most active of the zodiacs, enjoying any physical challenge Extremely organised and can easily multitask, they rely on facts rather than feelings or theories. They are brave and optimistic, especially in an apparent bad or difficult situation, though they are often impatient and very impulsive, with a short temper. Commanding, choleric and sometimes violent, but also adventurous, pioneering and extremely respected, although not always loved for their independence. They have a love for tattoos, piercings and faux leather.

Focusing on using the element of fire, they use a lot of candles in both their magic and also in just day to day life. Like their element of fire, they can also easily destroy and have a tendency to rush. Often being the culprit of wildfires. Using brute force when spellcasting rather than finesse. The flames they create also are able to advise and tell them what they need to know.

As well as using blood to perform magic when creating potions they use other bodily ingredients, such as hair, teeth and nails. They embrace all they meet but do not tolerate betrayal. They can easily make deals with devils and is always proud of their decision to do so. They don't require much to empower their magic, just their fiery passion, with the ability to tame the currents of energy around them. Their own blood is filled with waves of energy, ready to ignite the deepest desires. This allows them to easily charge magical weapons and loved ones with courage and positive energy to help them take on daunting challenges. Their magic is filled with courage and is often used to help bring about new beginnings.

- ARIES -
The Blood Witch

Quite a masculine witch, taking their own virility for granted. Self-absorbed, who often only concentrates on themselves, but they are not vain. A conqueror with a boisterous personality, they always take the lead in a romantic relationship, due to this they require an equally strong partner. A driving desire for competition, success and independence, their enthusiastic and hard-working nature makes them and their magic inclined to impulsiveness, irritability and immature behaviour.

With the power of their ruling planet Mars, which is the god of war and battle, they ignite fire everywhere they go. The fire they create is always pure, as it is the very first spark of ember and light. This spark lights up their path and inspires passion and courage where ever they go. Bold and fiercely determined, they spark enthusiasm and zealousness, their strength is like no other, with their own lack of fear also being somewhat of a magic power. They can activate and recharge powerful amulets and talismans. Their blood magic allows them to transfer vital energy to those in need, but this often comes with the price of sacrificing their own health. They are also skilled at banishing and exorcism, as their determined nature allows them to remove whatever is unwanted. However when their blood magic is used for evil they are capable of irreversible soul corruption.

- ARIES -
The Blood Witch

Marking: Left Wrist

Flowers: Thistle And Honey Suckle

Environment: Enjoys Being Surrounded By People In A City Centre Location, With Central Heating

Tools: Candles, Embers, Gold And Blood

Energy: Full Of Wild And Free Static Energy

Specialities: Master Of The Art Of Manifestation, Curses and Poppets. As Well As A Natural Pyrokinesis Ability

- FAMILIAR -
Silver Coyote

Quick thinking and loyal, with a beautiful silver fur coat that glistens brightly during full moons. Arriving in an Aries life with a smile, and a reminder not to take life too seriously. A trickster who is both playful and wise with a dutiful nature. The coyote familiar will help chase away gloomy clouds and negative energy by offering the gift of seeing life through eyes of good humour. Showing how to balance work and play, and how laughter is always a good medicine.

- TAURUS -
The Flower Witch
April 21 - May 21

A true and loyal friend who never tries to dominate. Competent at most things, but especially with earth-based activities, with the ability to succeed in spells for good fortune.

- TAURUS -
The Flower Witch

All of a Taurus witch's magic neither benefits nor harms and is highly physical when casting. Working with their hands they can easily make anything fertile and all flowers bloom in their presence. Although described as a flower witch, their magic comes from anything that grows, so they can gain power and energy from all plant types including trees and fungi. They enjoy knitting sweaters and keep detailed records and notes on everything. A known collector, who always wears clothes with lots of pockets. They use their advanced knowledge of plants to make potions and tinctures.

Extremely faithful and reliable, although at times quite stubborn and a little possessive, they are full of inner strength and incredibly courageous. They are very close with the spirits of the forest and make friends easily with nymphs, elves, and fae. Enjoying being surrounded by nature, so when they are in a more industrial environment they can feel anxious and suffer from panic and asthma attacks.

A good family person, that is headstrong, realistic but above all faithful, although prone to occasional violent outbursts. Peace loving and loyal they take their time and think things through before acting, being slow but sure especially in their walking pace. They have a taste for the good things in life and enjoy work and leisure to the full. Taking pleasure in food, drink, material possessions and affections. Although at time self-centred they are always extremely generous and responsible with money. Their open and friendly attitude makes them slow to respond to provocation, but when they do become angry others must beware. Strong minded, but they do not impose their own views on to others.

- TAURUS -
The Flower Witch

Ruled by the planet Venus, they can use their magic to charm and enchant. Their power is at it's most powerful in the spring and they are at their happiest when they have a big project or long incantation to work on. They have an extremely large healthy and verdant garden, filled with all manner of flowers and plant life. They have a talent for creating mojos to passively attract good luck and all blessings and need an appropriate amount of passionate energy to successfully perform any spell.

They experience life through all five of their senses, which intern creates a sensuality to their lifestyle and demeanour. Their magic helps the most when issues of trust and loyalty are at stake, and a Taurean witch will always be determined to get to the end of any endeavour, this can often make getting a stubborn Taurus to stop mid-spell casting almost impossible. Sometimes their magic can appear to just be blind luck, but they are so much more than that, it's just that good fortune and wealth come easily to them. This causes them to have a natural ability to make people feel safe when they are with them, and their home is always welcoming. They will always burn sage when entering a new place to remove any negative energy.

- TAURUS -
The Flower Witch

Marking:	Right Calf
Flowers:	Poppies And Foxgloves
Environment:	A Home Full Of Flowers And Coloured Glass
Tools:	Flowers, Wool, And Herbs
Energy:	Natural And Balanced Energy
Specialities:	Plant And Kitchen Magic, Botany, Ecology, As Well As Creating Powerful Mojos

- FAMILIAR -
Blind Jaguar

Strong like their witch, the blind jaguar makes their disability a strength, and has taught themselves to hear what cannot be seen. The jaguar familiar will compliment their master's magical ability with brute power, and with a strong spell resistance. Enjoys remaining in the shadows, so has a tendency to be most active during the night and sleeps during the day. Becoming very grumpy when their cat nap is disturbed, but once awake enjoys helping their master as best they can.

- GEMINI -
The Space Witch
May 22 - June 21

Their everyday magical powers are in their ability to communicate with almost everyone and their gift at social situations. They have strong telepathic skills and seem to know what other people are thinking.

- GEMINI -
The Space Witch

Unable to stand boredom, they spend their time either learning or teaching others. They are highly creative and quick-witted. Their magic involves communicating and they can talk to all manner of species, in particular with the fae folk. Due to this they always work in large covens. They make their own spells, usually verbal incantations, and surround themselves with books and knowledge of the stars.

Extremely intuitive and can easily sense changes in energy. Dual-natured and complex, they can be both outgoing and fun loving, as well as introverted and serious. Highly adaptable and intelligent, they have a love for freedom, but can often be held back by their own nervousness. Though their speciality is chakras, they are also proficient in voodoo, mind control, telekinesis, and pinning. As well as a having a passion for card reading and any form of magic that uses knowledge and guidance from the stars and astrology. Their element is air, which they use to cast spells to affect intellectual matters and communication. Due to their social skills, they can easily cast spells on large groups of people and can influence movements and travels. A Gemini witch can possess great telepathic abilities and they are most adept in Astral Projection. However they have to be really interested in what they are doing, otherwise, they lose focus and stop mid-process.

Though clever and imaginative they can be restless and prone to playing mind games and talking too much. During full moons, they work hard on divination and prophecy and prepare strong wishing spells. There love for communicating extends not just to their verbal magic but also written, and they create excellent spell books and manuscripts.

- GEMINI -
The Space Witch

Due to being ruled by the bright and ever-moving Mercury, they are the only witch that can freely travel to and from the underworld. Travelling through the dark corners of the psyche and back to Earth. With an out of this world mind, which is both mutable and flexible, continually switching back and forth between the right and left side of the brain, with them eventually mastering and using both sides simultaneously.

The Gemini witch is the most eclectic of all the signs, but also the most mercurial and fickle. They are skilled at ferreting out one's hidden enemies, but can also confuse the superficial for stability, and can sometimes jump to conclusions. They usually have so much going on in their lives that they tend to ignore their magical abilities, and therefore when compared to the other Horoscope Witches they use their magic powers the least.

With their space and stellar magic, they can perform extremely rare spells and feats, that manipulate space itself to a degree and utilise the stars and planets. They are also fully trained in astrokinetic combat, which fuses cosmic energy and physical combat. This grants them both vast power and flexibility, however despite making them extremely powerful it is also difficult to control and requires fine precision.

- GEMINI -
The Space Witch

Marking:	By Right Or Left Eye
Flowers:	Lavender And Lily Of The Valley
Environment:	Happiest When At A Museum Or Observatory
Tools:	Books, Stars, And Asteroids
Energy:	Nebula Energy
Specialities:	Expert In Chakras, And Has A Passion For Astrology And Meditation, They Also Specialise In Astral Projection, Telekinesis And Telepathy

- FAMILIAR -
Albino Boa Constrictor

A more traditional witch familiar, the albino boa constrictor regularly renews its skin and by doing this grants great transformation power to their master. The boa is also a strong healing ally, and also helps their master shed their fears and negative beliefs. The boa is also excellent at opening up Chakras, in particular, the Base Chakra or the 'Kundalini Awakening" which allows for understanding and the ability to embrace sacred sensuality in the body and spirit. With the help of the albino boa constrictor the rare and mystical become the norm, and what seems dangerous and powerful will help the Gemini witch achieve their goals.

- CANCER -

The Tea Witch

June 22 - July 22

Tenacious and highly imaginative, as well as very sentimental, which leaves them quite moody at times. They cast their spells and brew potions with lots of love and affection.

- CANCER -
The Tea Witch

The Cancer witch uses their magic a lot in the kitchen, enjoying using it to cook and bake, as well as to brew their own potions. Although human, they are distantly related to both werewolves and vampires. Due to this they love moonlight and work around the lunar cycles, with a deep understanding of astrology. They keep an intricate dream diary and often makes friends with ghosts and spirits, enjoying playing board games with them. Although challenging to get to know, once befriended they are extremely loyal. Their love for kitchen magic actually makes them quite the social asset as they know a great deal about good food and of course good tea. They also enjoy helping people that are going through a difficult time, especially young children.

A skilled conjurour who often conjures items for their own spells and rituals, and they always use boiled water in all their potions. The most powerful potion they make is a healing moon water potion, which can cure both physical and emotional injuries, but it should always be used sparingly and they never use it on themselves. They also use tides of the oceans to enchant some of their potions. At times they can seem mysterious, this is because they are a knower of secrets, and holding onto others confidences leaves them with sleepy eyes. Highly imaginative, they always plan for worst case scenario, this leaves them suspicious of others and quite insecure. However, this emotional side of them also allows them to be very sentimental and deeply intuitive. They love their home and the love that is given by family, in particular, that of motherly love, which leaves them governed by childhood memories. They are eternally blessed by the angels of their ancestors, hence why they have a number of gifts that were bestowed upon them at birth. Even though they show a

- CANCER -
The Tea Witch

hardness on the outside, they are actually soft on the inside and are in fact the gentlest and most fertile of all the Horoscope Witches, which can leave them vulnerable and easily hurt, that is why they use the mask of a tough and ultra-logical personality.

They solve problems with a tenacity of purpose and have an excellent memory. Their element is the element of water which reigns over emotions and love, and this is why spells of love and friendship are always perfectly completed by the Cancer witch. They are also excellent at using all forms of divination as they instinctively know what's going to happen, and would, in fact, make an excellent oracle, if only they would leave their own doubts and inertia behind.

In order for the Cancer witch to use their powers, they must feel safe and secure and must be reassured that no one will intrude or interrupt them, and don't particularly like being observed. Cancer magic supports comfort, the sort that comes from having a cosy warm home that is surrounded by loved ones, secure in the knowledge they are safe and not alone. The Cancer witch will always place a protection blessing on anywhere they call home, that way they can assure not only safety but also that their home is filled with prosperity, love and luck. Their psychic empathy can sense when a loved one is in pain and as a true mystic, they know just what they need, whether it be a family amulet of their great grandmother's tea leaves. They're always available to help anyone, with an open heart, solid advice, and with a warm cup of tea. However, when they get connected to someone else they need to watch out that they don't get overwhelmed with that person's emotions.

- CANCER -
The Tea Witch

Marking: Left Clavicle

Flowers: White Roses

Environment: Lives In Trees, But Prefers To Do Magic Indoors

Tools: Gossamer, Tea, Books, And Moonlight

Energy: Peaceful, Gentle And Matriarchal Energy

Specialities: Divination, Dream Magic, And A Great Conjuror And Astrologist

- FAMILIAR -
Twin Armadillos

These cheeky armadillos love company, having a happy family life and obviously a warm cup of their favourite herbal tea. With a strong outer armour they can roll into a ball in order to help support and defend their master, but also to get out of any chores or work they don't want to do. Like the Cancer witch they enjoy the element of water and as they the can hold their breath for over 6 minutes underwater they can often be found splashing about in a large bathtub. They both have very poor eyesight, but they make up for this with an amazing sense of smell and touch. Exceptional diggers they help their witch to plant herbs and plants to grow ingredients to make different tea and spells.

- LEO -
The Lava Witch
July 23 - August 22

Like the flames that they can create, they themselves are bright and courageous, someone who is a born leader with a warm heart, making them a natural enchanter that can easily charm and hypnotise others into getting their own way.

- LEO -
The Lava Witch

Blessed by the sun, the Leo witch works best during the daytime. As a lava witch they often use fire-based magic. They are quite social and they enjoy being in a small close-knit coven. Incredible at visualisation allowing them to make their own dreams become a reality. They make their own spells and have skilled hands and a strong voice that carries a spark. Always adorned in precious gems and also has wild untamed hair. A less traditional witch, they use incense, herbs and flames when incanting and spell casting. At times quite forcefull, they use extremely active and offensive magic, with their own energy being very open, raw and animalistic. An extrovert with an incredibly strong presence and great magnetism that leaves them with a need to dominate. It also makes them enjoy being in the spotlight, enjoying praise and never hovering at the back of the stage. This is because they are confident of their own abilities and also their own sex appeal. Often leaving them both loved and loathed simultaneously by others.

At their best, they are a splendid leader, but at their worst, they are a vain and bullying bore. Self-assured, they enjoy a life of luxury and being pampered, in particular spas with volcanic hot springs. They love having a cause or a mission, this makes them the most likely of all the Horoscope Witches to accept and go on a quest. They do well on any quest that allows them to be the centre of attention. On quests, they are at times impatient, but always organised and offers an unquestioning assurance to others. Incredibly magnanimous, but ruthless to those who challenge them. Always ready to start a revolution, they are positive, strong-willed and idealistic. They are ambitious and proud and this sometimes can leave them a little selfish, and unaware of others feelings when trying to reach a goal. But generally, they are valiant, step-firm and mind courteous.

- LEO -
The Lava Witch

Talented at casting spells that expand fame or popularity and for enhancing all kinds of pleasures. The Leo witch performs best when they have realised their own divine origin, they need to feel like royalty, or like they're someone important. Highly dependable, they will always get things done. Finding the best way to fix a problem, and doing so with flair and confidence. Whether they need to or not, they will always take control of a situation, but not out of spite. Usually, they genuinely believe they are helping and doing the best for the situation.

Thriving in adversity, they would never leave their comrades behind on purpose, in fact, they enjoy having the company, and will always share the credit, as long as they get plenty of praise too. It's always great to have them on your side, otherwise, they make for a fearsome enemy. Naturally wise, as well as kind and benevolent, they may at times stray to the dark side, but they tend to have enough self-discipline not to succumb completely. They get restless when forced into routine and hate limiting their activities for the sake of safety and prudence. They also hate pettiness and closed minded people. Leo witches have a confident energy that makes their magic able to inspire courage in others, with the intention of most of the spells that they cast being to help or improve other people lives, rather than their own. Their laugh is infectious and their authenticity is their greatest power, and it makes them extremely captivating and fascinating which increase their ability to charm others easily.

- LEO -
The Lava Witch

Marking:	Upper Right Arm
Flowers:	Marigolds And Sunflowers
Environment:	Prefers Urban And City Environments
Tools:	Incense, Herbs, Precious Gems, And Fire
Energy:	Active, Offensive And Animalistic Energy
Specialities:	Talented Illusionist, Who Is Highly Skilled In Enchantment, Divination, And Fate Alteration. They Were Also Born With A Natural Pyrokinesis Ability

- FAMILIAR -
Rare Red Tiger

The rare red fur of this tiger makes this familiar extra lucky and is highly prized by others. The tiger is fiercely loyal, curious and, like it's master, it is extremely charismatic. They are always there when their witch is in need of reassurance or needs help living up to their greatest potential. The tiger will only like others who show respect towards them, and will teach their master patience and will not allow them to procrastinate, and they are always willing to lend a powerful paw to help keep their witch going.

- VIRGO -
The Forest Witch
August 23 - September 23

Since helping people and fixing things that are broken are strong concerns for the Virgo witch, it's not surprising that much of their magical ability has to do with healing and turning chaos into peace.

- VIRGO -
The Forest Witch

Known for their restless minds and busy hands, the Virgo witch has become a master of manipulating energy and is very physical when performing spells. They always do their magic while surrounded by trees, and are friends with all the local plants and animals. Though they appear quite shy, they enjoy keeping a blog for other to read in order for them to get to know them better. Hardworking, kind and peaceful. Dedicated to their craft, they are logical about everything they do, but their over analysing tendencies can turn them into an over thinker and worrier.

They appear to admit a natural glow and enjoy wearing clothes made with denim when exploring. They were born with the natural ability to heal most people, animals, plants, and also the earth. A bit of a hermit, they need time for themselves in order to recharge their magic. Ruled by the wise and practical planet Mercury they are mutable and have highly pedantic views, but are also intelligent precise and observant, making them a practical supporter of order. Mercury is cerebral, whereas the moon is emotional; this can be a source of either conflict or harmony for their spells, depending on the desired outcome. Critically inclined and patient, without an ounce of flamboyance in their body. They have a shrill voice and are prone to brevity, they are exceedingly well spoken and judicious, a witty but discreet soul. They are studious and enjoy learning about history, which has taught them to combine intelligence and common sense. At times they hoard things, but also sometimes they can also be obsessed with cleanliness, precision and neatness. They are rarely capable of really letting go, and prefers honest recognition of achievements to idle flattery.

- VIRGO -
The Forest Witch

Supportive, loving, and a magical multitasker. They dislike unskilled work and enjoy imposing order on chaos, with ruthless analytical prowess. Their natural philosophy makes them a genius for intellectual discrimination. Although their element is Earth, they are almost always lost in responsibilities trying to figure out how to serve and fulfil the needs of others. A blue sky uplifts their mood and reminds them of their divine origin, which is their true nature, free of obligations. The Virgo witch is miraculous when dealing with spells for healing and any kind of evolution, either material or spiritual. Because of their natural ability to deal with many issues and people at the same time they can do miracles in telepathy and peace spells.

For a Virgo to activate their magical powers they need to remember they come from a divine source and aren't just flesh and bones. In addition, they need to try their best to focus on the bright side of life and to leave their fears and doubts behind. Being a perfectionist, they except the best from themselves and everyone they deal with. This can lead to them being very nitpicky and critical, but this also causes them to be very reliable and industrious. With a strong sense of responsibility and honour, they are extremely hard working. The Virgo witch lends helpful energy to spells and indeed mundane activities as well. Devoted to building a firm foundation, including planning and organisational activities, anything that requires a lot of research, and even the most minutiae task that could make difference between success and failure. The most fastidious intellectual of the Horoscope Witches, making them excellent at casting spells requiring great attention to detail. Spells worked for mental prowess, stability and conscientiousness take deep roots when cast by them. The more a Virgo witch learns and grows, the more their magical powers evolve.

- VIRGO -
The Forest Witch

Marking:	Right Side Of Neck
Flowers:	Buttercups
Environment:	Lives Deep Inside Forests
Tools:	Herbs, Succulents, Crystals, And Denim
Energy:	Earth And Herbal Energy
Specialities:	Expert In Botany, As Well As Growth, Banishment, Telepathy And Cleansing Magic. Has The Natural Ability To Heal Anything Living

- FAMILIAR -
One-Antlered Deer

This familiar helps their master to be more compassionate towards others and, more importantly, towards themselves. Their missing antler gains their witch greater regeneration and renewal powers. Always alert they remain mindful and diligently aware while their Virgo witch gets distracted by the finer details. With tenderness and strength, the one-antlered deer is there when obstacles challenge the path, teaching their witch how to remain gentle, determined and sure even in difficult situations. Remembering that a gentle soul is not a helpless one.

- LIBRA -
The Music Witch
September 24 - October 23

|

With a strong magical power when it comes to making things harmonious, and for bringing people together in a positive way. They are able to achieve balance in relationships within their own lives, and balance within their own body.

- LIBRA -
The Music Witch

With an immense enjoyment of life, the Libra witch lives each day to the full. Born with a strong connection to sound, they sing and compose their own spells, and have an extraordinary talent for playing, creating and inventing musical instruments. Their magic not only empowers themselves but also anyone else who hears it being cast. Blessed with inspiration, they are talented not only in music but in all the arts. They use their music to summon demons and mythical creatures to do their bidding. With cold skin and a smell of expensive perfume, they are much much stronger than they look. Always logical, devoted, and extremely social, with a gracious and fair mind. These traits make them remarkably diplomatic and also excellent mediators in any situation.

The Libra witch often uses their element of air, and the very winds around them to perform powerful rituals. At times indecisive, they sometimes use illusions to hide the truth, but only as a last resort as they want nothing more than to be liked by others, and automatically likes anyone they meet. Gentle, and tolerant, they are very easy to get along with. They have balanced moderate views and are instantly repelled by extremism of any kind. Their chief failing is being too easily influenced due to their social and courteous nature. The most feminine and cultured of the Horoscope Witches, they are exceedingly charming and, when needed, knows how to use their charms to get what they want. Gaining a great deal of happiness from a satisfactory home life. However, when at home they can be rather lazy and aren't very industrious. With work that involves strenuous and physical effort having very little appeal to them. This is because they have such an easy-going, relaxed attitude. As a peacemaker, they love harmony not only in life but in all the sounds and music they surround themselves with.

- LIBRA -
The Music Witch

They have a natural talent for beauty and glamour spells, this is because this type of spell requires a lot of creativity, which they have an abundance of. They are also miraculous when dealing with peace spells and spells that achieve balance, especially when affecting relationships. A Libra witch's powers are at their strongest when the Libra focuses on their own self-belief and truly believes they are the ultimate enchanter. Always the champion of the underdog due to their empathetic and sympathetic nature. Often tending to the needs of others before they tend to themselves, making them the ultimate team player. They adore replenishing their magical energy by going to concerts or to the theatre or opera.

As a true child of Venus they are socially curious, utterly charming, but also extremely compassionate and able to compromise even in the most difficult of situations. A real social chameleon, and at times hard to read, they can easily blend in and reflect their surroundings be it physically with a glamour or illusion, or mentally with the use of conversation and song. Venus also rules romance, this gives the Libra witch a natural skill at magic related to love, as well as spells that require diplomacy and adaptability. They also have a natural magic when it comes to looking good, and are admired for how beautifully they cast spells.

- LIBRA -
The Music Witch

Marking:	Left Shoulder
Flowers:	Bluebells
Environment:	Seeks Out Covens And Other Witches
Tools:	Perfume, Incense, Instruments And Salt
Energy:	Peaceful Energy, Gaining Power From The Air And Winds
Specialities:	Rituals, Summonings, Healing, Glamours, And Illusions

- FAMILIAR -
A Fluffle Of Rabbits

The Libra witch is the only witch who's familiar continually changes in number, often increasing to over hundred their fluffle of rabbits fills their home in order to keep them company and to stop them feeling lonely. However when on a quest or mission they will only take a few of their rabbit companions with them. Rabbits teach their master to look before they leap, and suit their Libra master because they too are creative problem solvers. They are experts at monitoring rituals, and can navigate sounds as easily as their witch creates them.

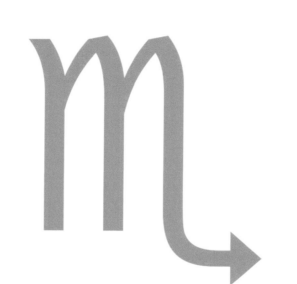

- SCORPIO -

The Night Witch

October 24 - November 22

Some would say that the Scorpio witch is, in fact, the most powerful of the Horoscope Witches as they have so many magical powers that are both positive and negative. It is almost shocking what they can manifest and do when they put their mind to it.

- SCORPIO -
The Night Witch

The Scorpio witch is highly traditional and completely nocturnal, doing most things after midnight, as they are most inspired and enlightened at in the darkness. Enjoying the silence and blackness. With their dark eyes and darker nails, they frequent graveyards and learn from the ghosts and spirits living there. Wisest of all the Horoscope Witches, their magic is traditional and defensive and is cast using strong emotions and during energetic weather. With powerful instincts and a resourceful personality. They are loyal, focused, but also solitary and stubborn. Hiding their own fears, but this allows them to easily able to see through lies. Being tenacious in love and driven by the urge for power, they enjoy hard work and have serious attitude, which can often turn into extreme competitiveness and authoritarianism that often brings them a lot of success. Enjoying most anything that involves close and detailed research and spell casting.

With a variety of interests, they enjoy opportunities to test their magical strength. Their strong psychic abilities, they are highly skilled at using pendulums and tarot cards. They focus on defensive magic, which makes them susceptible to attacks. Despite their defensive nature, however, they can quickly bite back when provoked. Quiet and haunted, they are afraid of sleep, especially if made to sleep at night. So they are prone to insomnia, but not to worry as they are reborn with new energy every new moon. Knowing and a great keeper of promises, they will help anyone for a price. Secrets and gossip ignite their curiosity, and they can easily see what is hidden due to their powerful instincts. Cunning and brave, their stubbornness often makes them hide their true emotions and fears, but this actually makes them talented at spirit work and possession. The Scorpio witch is great when manipulating energy and this is why they can create

- SCORPIO -
The Night Witch

powerful magic charms and sigils. Their instincts are almost always correct and are closely linked to their excellent survival skills. If cast at night their spells and incantations are extra powerful and along with defensive magic they can also create strong banishment spells and are skilled at removing obstacles. Due to their nature to adapt easily to every new environment, they are also good when it comes to spells that have to do with change. The best time to activate their powers is when they're alone and in private, and once they have tapped into their own instincts, the more primitive, the better. This helps them ensure that they remain focused on the matter at hand.

Ruled by the planet Mars, they can appear sinister and have forbidding reputation, due to at times being slightly deceitful. Passionate and with a wholly original creativity that at times comes across as a bit morbid. They are difficult to get along with because of their jealous nature, their secretiveness, their fierce willpower, and also their strong likes and dislikes. They take a long time to make up their mind about whether they like someone or not, however once befriended they are loyal and honest and remain a lifelong companion. Intensely conscious of their self-integrity, with a keen sense of personal pride. And like with their relationships once committed to a task or quest they rarely change course, however when they do change their minds about something they do so abruptly and violently. They never set out to please, but despite this, they are usually very good company. Their magic energy supports incantations related to increasing psychic ability, contacting other planes, merging with a Deity, and spirituality, as well as knowledge of past lives and reincarnation. Along with the planet Mars the Scorpio witch is also

- SCORPIO -
The Night Witch

influenced by Pluto, who is the God of the underworld and represents transformation, hence their extreme passions and impenetrable mind. Highly intuitive they are a natural mind reader. Their obsseions stem from their emotional intensity, which at times can be overwhelming to those around them. They are either the lightest light or the darkest dark. There is no in between with them. Their work is often linked to the dead, and the spirit world, making theim very compatable with almlst all lunar spellwok which allows them to give and recive messages with the spirits.

Marking:	Right Hand
Flowers:	Dark Red Carnations
Environment:	They Can Make A Home Anywhere As Long As They Have Privacy
Tools:	Pendulums, Tarot Cards, And Bones
Energy:	Embraces Dark Energy
Specialities:	Clairvoyance, Spirit Work, Mind Reading, And Possession

- FAMILIAR -
Flightless Crow

The original messenger of mortality, the crow familiar, despite being flightless, makes for an excellent spy and helps it's master to hunt out prized secrets and hidden objects. A teacher who helps the Scorpio witch to gain power and wisdom through social connection and resourcefulness. An extremely traditional familiar for such a traditional type of witch, the crow can easily cross between the spiritual and material world so can readily support their witch whenever they travel between realms.

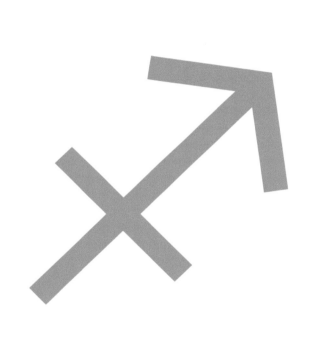

- SAGITTARIUS -
The Lightning Witch
November 23 - December 21

So laid back they neither care for offensive or defensive magic. Instead enjoys using their magic to play and amuse, and they love the expressions they cause on children's faces when they prove to them that magic is real.

- SAGITTARIUS -
The Lightning Witch

Always smiling and laughing, the Sagittarius witch has wide eyes, chapped lips, and an open personality. They attend as many witches' sabbaths as possible. Known for using a lot of energy and physical movement when casting their spells, and for being extremely reckless at riding their broom. A known trickster, who is passionate about everything they do. Extremely curious and eager to learn and explore, but also easily distracted, and never stays still for very long. They love bright neon colours and also collecting moonlight. As well as being an avid collector of rainwater, snow, or anything that is leftover by a storm.

Their ruling planet is Jupiter, which makes them a child of Zeus and Thor, and it is this that makes them so talented and powerful with lightning and with all storm based magic in general. Their magic can become exceptionally powerful during bad weather when they have lots of focused currents of energy to use, but they never use this power for evil or destruction. Instead, they are always very wise and fair. Jupiter also blesses them with the ability to be a source of happiness and optimism, so they are great at healing negativity. The Sagittarius witch can tap into spiritual wisdom, almost any time they want, and access information which is prohibited. Jupiter is also the planet of abundance, healing and expansion; ergo they are often referred to as the wanderer of the Horoscope Witches. They will push themselves further both physically and mentally than any other Horoscope Witch and are able to break chains with both their wisdom and optimism. Their own personal drive and need for freedom make them excellent at transformation spells and despite their recklessness they are actually very skilled at flying, and with any spell that affects travel for that matter. As well as having a skill for spells that help others travel to other realms.

- SAGITTARIUS -
The Lightning Witch

Loyal and intelligent and if need be rebelious, the Sagittarius witch is very motherly but never possessive, and also an absolute genius when it comes to communication. They will succeed at any skilled or even unskilled task as they are prepared to tackle any challenge as long as it leaves them a certain amount of freedom, with a resolve to meet problems head-on. They have overwhelming vitality, determination and dogged persistence, they have a passion for meeting the challenge of a problem. When in charge they are good-natured leaders, with a considerable ability to get things done, and are usually on the side of the oppressed. Using their positive attitude to heal and neutralize negativity and pain.

Generous and idealistic, in social situations especially with other witches they are very extroverted and enthusiastic. They are prone to success and have a skill at controlling their own and others fate, with the ability to incant spells that give more than one opportunity to achieve a certain goal. Talented at most things, and interested in almost everything. Often wasting their talents in too many fields, and at times become a bit of a bragger. Their natural outspoken and straightforward demeneer often causes people to pick quarrels with them, and it also makes them a bit promiscuous. Although they are extremely lovable, they themselves often resist the love that is offered to them, for fear of losing their freedom. They love animals and are excellent at horse riding, and any activity that takes place outside, as they see homelife as dull.

The key for a Sagittarius witch to activate their power is optimism, they need to feel the spark of happiness in their hearts. Feeling that every little thing is going to be alright allows them to truly control the energy around them. Their optimism

- SAGITTARIUS -
The Lightning Witch

can be somewhat over-the-top at times, but that's where their power truly lies. Nothing is impossible in their eyes, and they believe there is always something waiting for them on the other side of the horizon. A non-conformist when it comes to magic, they are often found experimenting with new spells and ritual methods and working on the most elusive types of magic. They seem to make magic happen wherever they go.

Marking:	Right Cheek
Flowers:	Carnations
Environment:	They Can Make A Home Anywhere As Long As They Have Privacy
Tools:	Electric Currents & Rainwater
Energy:	Combines Their Own Energy With The Weather. Leaving Their Magic Erratic And Spontaneous
Specialities:	Obscure Crafts, Dead Languages, & Transformation Potions

- FAMILIAR -
Toothless Otter

This familiar belongs to those who see life as a playground. Actually a very sensible animal most of the time, but has the distinct ability to know when to play and how to find renewed joy in life that balances out more serious matters. They help to teach their master to stop fighting against adversity. Always up for an adventure, like their witch, the otter lets curiosity direct them. They never worry about what is left behind, instead always look forward, never getting locked in the quagmire of worry.

- CAPRICORN -
The Soil Witch
December 22 - January 20

Often to be found alone, wearing a warm woollen jumper that they have knitted themselves, the Capricorn witch has a great power over the Earth and its soils and can make even the driest and most barren land rich with nutrients.

- CAPRICORN -
The Soil Witch

The Capricorn witch is a solitary witch, practising their magic alone and in private. They have their own herb garden and a vast collection of stones, and focus mainly on tangible and traditional spells. They enjoy speaking to animals and plants over humans. Easily able to assert their magical dominance, and with the very rare times they are made angry the ground itself is left trembling. Extremely logical, responsible and patient, they never waste or rush anything, and are always completely prepared. However, their faithful nature makes them extremely unforgiving and they will hold a grudge for all eternity. Their magic actually comes from when the stars and planets allign, and they have the strongest energy during eclipses and other rare astrological events. They focus mainly on defence and protection magic and fill their home with scrawlings, carving, and sigils to protect from strangers and danger. When they rarely attend a coven gathering or witches' sabbath, most other witches there remain distant and silent in their presence out of fear and awe. With love and a great deal of discipline they can command elemental forces, and they produce everything they make with top quality craftsmanship and care. Reserved, uncommunicative and with a lot of self-discipline, the Capricorn witch is the most traditional of all the Horoscope Witches and is a diplomatic asset during times of need and conflict. However, they do not get on very well with anyone overbearing and enthusiastic and does their best to avoid alchol, as they always like to have full control over themselves and any situation. Full of wit and calmness, though at times subject to pessimism and melancholy, they are extremely introverted and self-effacing. Despite this, however, they are extremely ambitious, and burn with the desire to succeed, and have an extreme almost crippling fear of failure. They never seek success in a dramatic way. Instead, they take on long painstaking

- CAPRICORN -
The Soil Witch

struggles and quests that others would have just ignored, but this trait often takes them to the top. They have an unbending approach to any task and it's this rigidity that both attracts and repels other witches. They are in fact intensely competitive, even though they try to hide it, with them commanding respect from people rather than affection, as they enjoy being in a position of power. Loyal and astute, they use a glamour to protect themselves with a hard outward appearance. They can succeed in most spells, as the key to unlocking their magical powers is a strong determination to succeed, this is shown by how once they've made their mind up about something they tend to achieve it. Ruled by the wise and strong Saturn, the Capricorn witch can perform miracles when it comes to wealth and completing objectives, and have a natural ability to find ways to fulfil goals and satisfy their own ambition. With the help from Saturn, they are also talented at tapping into the wisdom of their ancestors and ancient magic. With the help of Saturn can easily uncover past-lives and overcome any past negative influences. Sometimes the most magical thing about them is how wise beyond their years they are.

Never really happy when confined or surrounded by lots of people, they are good at most things, excelling at monotonous tasks, due to their passion for detail and exactness. They put all their effort and determination into making something accurate, this makes them a very good imitator. They have grown up to have self-reliance, respect for convention, and a dry subtle sense of humour, they have a deep love for beauty and can see beauty in absolutely everything, except themselves. They enjoy order, so love schedules, creating to-do lists, and are rarely late and have no patience for others who don't show up on time.

- CAPRICORN -
The Soil Witch

They are a remarkably loyal friend, who would go to the end of the Earth for a loved one. Due to their sentimental nature, they like to feel needed and can put themselves in a very unhappy place this way. They do have the ability however to handle anything, even though they may be totally panicked under the surface, they would never let it show. Always able to formulate a plan quickly, even in the most stressful of situations. Due to their own despondency and at times depression they need to always avoid divination, and should instead work on grounding rituals.

Marking:	Left Foot
Flowers:	Pansies And Ivy
Environment:	Lives Happily By Themselves In A Moss Covered Stone Cottage
Tools:	Rich Soil, Wool, And Jars Of Salt
Energy:	Gets Their Energy From The Earth Itself
Specialities:	Defence & Protection Magic, Especially Sigils And Runes

- FAMILIAR -
200 Year Old Tortoise

This old and wise tortoise teaches its witch to remain true to their path and to make peace with their choices. It reminds the Capricorn witch that the key to overcoming obstacles is strength and determination, and helps them carry the burdens they have when they take too much on at once. The tortoise also helps with grounding rituals, returning into its shell to meditate, and also when in danger. They help their master when under attack and improve any defence magic and sigils incanted by their witch.

- AQUARIUS -
The Modern Witch
January 21 - February 19

At times they can seem a little quirky, as they are willing to step out of their comfort zone for something that is important to them. The universe blessed them with an eccentric point of view, and that is their biggest superpower.

- AQUARIUS -
The Modern Witch

At the forefront of all new magic, the Aquarius witch enjoys collecting any gadgets they can find and then uses them in their rituals and incantations. They are also highly skilled at writing magic into code and text. They use a lot of different methods of magic and love exploring different techniques, with incantations being their overall favourite method. They always try and adapt their spells to feel unique and one of a kind. Ruled by Saturn and Uranus they are ethereal, idealistic and emotional, this makes them inclined to devote themselves to causes, especially charitable ones. With the freedom of others being as important to them as their own freedom. Uranus is also the planet of chaos and unexpected change, this has caused them to become a bit of a social rebel, with a gifted mind that is progressive and futuristic, with them often able to bring different worlds together simply by just being themselves. They have a spiritual awareness through meditation and yoga.

Highly progressive they balance their magic well with science, making them fond of innovation and reforms, with no respect for convention or tradition. They take an intellectual approach to life, but this never makes them cold or unemotional. A strong believer in sexual equality, and often active in covens formed for a social cause or political reform or for the protection of the environment. They are very open-minded and are always willing to listen to other points of view. However, they also have a reputation for being tactless and sometimes obstinate. Inspired to a higher consciousness, this can often come across as air-headedness and thought without action, which at times is actually true. As they do have a tendency to allow their mind to wander aimlessly in the vast pseudo-intellectual wilderness.

- AQUARIUS -
The Modern Witch

The Aquarius witch is talented at inventing and creating new things from seemingly nothing. Their creativity being just as powerful as their magical powers, as is their ability to liberate and break free from anything that imposes upon their freedom. Connected with the air, they often speak to birds, who gift them feathers. They love playing in the rain and dancing in storms and are always collecting raindrops for spells, and enjoy learning form clouds. This often leaves their hair full of leaves and wind. Their feet are also often left dirty, but their mind is clean and sharp. Tending to work by themselves and known as a bit of a hermit, proudly marching to the beat of their own drum. However, they are still able to interact well with others and never feel alone. A born humanitarian, who is a brilliant listener. Passionate and independent, but also incredibly uncompromising and sometimes temperamental. A collector of many things, keeping trinkets and mementoes in small jars. Sometimes their magic is as soft as a summer rain and other times cold as hail, they are known to ask for a lot of favours. They are completely free of vanity, and yet intensely conscious of their dignity. An adventurous approach to life, the Aquarius witch hates to be dominated and believes it is important to be an individual. With themselves having an originality and genius for inventiveness. They are excellent at performing spells that liberate and break any kinds of bonds and attachments. Their thirst for freedom empowers them to break negative spells, curses and addictions. They also have a great natural ability for astral projection and remote viewing. Just because the Aquarius' body is in bed asleep, doesn't mean that their spirit is there too. With the places they can travel to in their spiritual-being being vast and unlimited. The key to unlocking their magical power is for them to always remain free and unique and to always take deep breaths of air when panicked.

- AQUARIUS -
The Modern Witch

Marking:	Right Rib Cage
Flowers:	Orchids
Environment:	Enjoys Being Anywhere They Can Help Others
Tools:	Raindrops, Gadgets, Burlap, And Feathers
Energy:	Electric Star Energy
Specialities:	Palmistry, Foresight, Tea Leaf Reading, Incarnations, Astral Projection, And Divination

- FAMILIAR -
Golden True Owl

Belonging to the witch that finds wisdom in silence, the Golden True Owl teaches its master how to see the truth and helps them to have courage when it is time for them to face their demons. The owl is also skilled at seeing things from a spiritual perspective, from its vantage points it can allow their witch to open doorways into other realms and to connect with Devas, Ancestors, Angels and the Divine, all due to having such a strong connection with the element of air. However the owl familiar cannot be deceived, so does not tolerate magic to do with illusions or secrets.

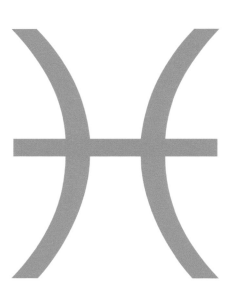

- PISCES -

The Sea Witch

February 20 - March 20

A cosmic hybrid of the entire zodiac wheel, they are the Horoscope Witch of universal oneness and divinity. Their intuition is godlike and their heart is overflowing with compassion, they are truly mystical being.

- PISCES -
The Sea Witch

Smelling of salt, often wearing pearls, and with deep misty eyes filled with empathy, the Pisces witch is often to be found out on open water. They use ocean water in all their magic to scry, purify, and sanctify. Outgoing and kind, they can easily make friends with fairies, and often meddles in the fairy world. Known as a peaceful humanitarian, who is gentle, compassionate and strong-willed. Although a very friendly person, they are overly trusting and can be easily hurt.

Ruled by Jupiter and Neptune, they are visionaries, with an amazing intuition and skill at evasion, which also makes them a talented actor. However, they do lack decisiveness and staying power and are known to drop out of a quest last minute. Despite this, however, they are always lovable and loving. With the power granted to them by Neptune, the planet of compassion and subconscious realms, they are eternally travelling between space and time. Despite living in our world, they actually belong to another, never feeling 100% okay with life in the material world, and always feeling like they are missing a great truth, which leaves them constantly trying to find that place where they truly fit in. Often retiring from the real world to a place of their own creation using hallucinations. They are able to perform miracles when dealing with spells to do with other worlds, and can successfully meddle with the dream world and manipulate dreams to promote intuition and divination. Illusions being their primary power, with their strongest illusions being for healing and empowerment in others. A true empath, who can look straight into someone's soul, and appear to know a person better than they know themselves. Although their own head is often full of crashing waves, so they can struggle to understand what they themselves want. Nonetheless, they are

- PISCES -
The Sea Witch

overflowing with magic and wonder, allowing them to easily transcend the physical plane. A truly sweet witch who can easily invite the shyest and most allusive magical creature into their lives, and can establish a firm and fruitful connection with the spirit of nature.

Using all natural things from the ocean in their magic practices, not just the water, items such as seashells, salt and driftwood. They use these items to create magical offerings for all the sea deities they worship. Although they prefer the use of ocean water, as their element is water they can use any form of it, and often collect rainwater and then cleanse it beneath the light of the full moon. And they will even bottle their own tears and keep them for spells so as not to waste anything. With their magic mainly focusing on healing, growth and defence.

The Pisces witch is an idealist, who is amiable, and at times vague and even sometimes devious. They have an easy going attitude towards life, and are liable to be easily influenced by others and sometimes even being labelled as a conformist. They are the complete opposite of egotistical, and always oppose material values for spiritual. Soft and gentle, they can be submissive and are often left anxious to please, although they never want to be bullied, and instead avoids confrontation with guile rather than outright opposition. Not naturally a hard worker, as they can lack motivation, ambition or a need for power. Instead, they have a passionate power to serve fellow humans and will work hard for a cause they believe in despite their lack of dynamism. Although receptive they have hyper sensitivity and do no take kindly to outside attempts at regimentation.

- PISCES -
The Sea Witch

Marking:	Left Outer Thigh
Flowers:	Water Lilies
Environment:	Lives Close To The Coast And Enjoys Being Out On Open Water
Tools:	Seashells, Ocean Water, And Crystals
Energy:	Healing, Spiritual, And Defensive
Specialities:	Astral Travel, Healing, Divination, Hallucinations, Illusions, & Potion Making, As Well As Knowledgeable Of Crystal Balls & Divine Rods

- FAMILIAR -
Pink Nosed Polar Bear

The Pink Nosed Polar Bear is notoriously fearless this is because, not only does its pink nose make it harder for it to hide away, but also because their master needs the reassurance they provide. They also offer introspection and help their witch to navigate emotional waters with clarity. They offer the Pisces witch protection and strength when they undertake dream or spirit work or when they just feel weak or helpless, and help them to be more patient and persistent. The polar bear also receives veneration as a sage and educator in its own right.

- EPILOGUE -

Thank you for taking the time to read Horoscope Witches, I sincerely hope you have enjoyed getting to know each of the Witches and that you liked and hopefully were able to relate to your own Horoscope.

Over several months I completed a character design challenge, where I had to create a witch persona (or witchsona) for each of the twelve horoscope signs. Using each horoscope's stereotypical traits and dispositions to create each witch, along with an appropriate familiar and magic type. This book is the accumulation of this personal project and contains not only the illustrations I created, but also the researched character profiles that I created and used when designing each Horoscope Witch.

Hopefully, the future will see the creation of more art books filled with quirky characters and fun stories that will be able to be shared with the world. Thank you again for reading this book and I hope you have a happy and magic filled life!

- ABOUT THE AUTHOR -

Nona

The artist Nona was born and resides in the city of Liverpool in the UK. Graduating from University with a Bachelor of Science in Computer Engineering. A self-taught artist, she has since had the pleasure of working on several illustration projects, as well as several ongoing personal projects and art books. She has had work exhibited and sold across Europe, North America and Australia, and currently has work on permanent display at the Bluecoat Chambers, Liverpool. With a passion for art, technology, and travel, Nona currently fits her drawing and painting around her day job and home life, with the hope that one day her passion for creating art and stories will become her full-time career.

Social Media: @nonaGalleryArt
Website: www.nonaGallery.com

- GLOSSARY -

Amiable - Having or displaying a friendly or pleasant manner.

Amulet - An ornament or small piece of jewellery thought to give protection against evil and danger.

Ancestor - A person from whom one is descended.

Angel - A spiritual being believed to act as an agent of a God.

Astral Projection/Travel - The method in which an individual can separate their consciousness from their physical body.

Astrokinetic Combat - The power to fuse cosmic energy and physical combat, granting them both vast power and flexibility to use several different powers.

Astrology - The study of the movement and relative positions of the celestial bodies interpreted as having an influence on human affairs and on the natural world.

Banishment - The act of getting rid of something unwanted.

Benevolent - Well-meaning and Kindly.

Botany - The scientific study of plants.

Burlap - Material woven from jute, hemp or similar fibre.

Capricious - Given to sudden and unaccountable changes of mood or behaviour.

Celestial Bodies - Any natural body outside of the Earth's atmosphere.

Chakra - One of seven centres of spiritual power in the human body.

Choleric - Bad-tempered or irritable

Clairvoyance - The ability to perceive things or events in the future or beyond normal sensory contact.

Conjure - Cause something to appear by means of a magical ritual.

- GLOSSARY -

Cosmic Energy - See Shakti

Coven - A group or meeting of witches.

Crystal Ball - A solid globe of glass or crystal that is used in fortune telling.

Curse - A solemn utterance intended to invoke a supernatural power to inflict harm or punishment on someone or something.

Deity - A god or goddess.

Demons - An evil spirit or devil.

Devas - A member of a class of divine beings in the Vedic period, that can be both benevolent and evil.

Devil - A supreme spirit of evil.

Divination - The practice of seeking knowledge of the future or the unknown by supernatural means.

Divine Rods - A stick or rod used for dowsing.

Dowsing - A technique for searching for underground water or anything invisible be observing the motion of a pointer.

Eclipse - An obscuring of the light from one celestial body by the passage of another between it and the observer.

Ecliptic - A great circle on the celestial sphere representing the sun's apparent path during the year.

Ecology - A branch of biology that deals with the relations of organisms to one another and their physical surroundings.

Elemental - Related to embodying one several powers of nature.

Enlightened - Being spiritually aware.

Elf - An elusive supernatural creature in human form with pointed ears, magical powers and a capricious nature.

Enchanter - A person who uses magic or sorcery, especially to put someone or something under a spell.

Ethereal - Extremely delicate and light in a way that seems not to be of this world.

Exorcism - The expulsion of a supposed evil spirit from a person or place.

- GLOSSARY -

Fae - A young fairy.

Fairy - A small magical sprite with insect-like wings, that usually either grants wishes or wreaks mischief.

Familiar - A magic user's spiritual helper manifested in an animal form.

Feat - An achievement that requires great courage, skill, or strength.

Foresight - The ability to predict what will happen or be needed in the future.

Ghosts - An apparition of a dead person which is believed to appear to the living.

Glamour - Enchantment or illusion that is used to disguise a person or object.

Gossamer - A fine substance consisting of cobwebs spun by small spiders.

Hallucination - An experience involving the apparent perception of something not present.

Hermit - A person living in solitude.

Horoscope - A forecast of a person's future, typically including a delineation of character and circumstances, based on the relative positions of the stars and planets at the time of that person's birth.

Hypnosis - The induction of a state of consciousness in which a person apparently loses the power of voluntary auction and is then highly responsive to suggestion.

Illusionist - A person who performs tricks that deceive the eye.

Incantation - A series of words said as a magic spell or charm.

Incense - A spice or other substance that is burned for the sweet smell it produces.

Introspection - The examination or observation of one's own mental and emotional processes.

Jute - A rough fibre made from stems of a tropical Old World plant.

Kundalini Awakening - Allows a person to experience deeper empathy with others and this empathy can become almost telepathic.

- GLOSSARY -

Manifestation - An event or action that clearly shows or embodies something abstract or theoretical.

Meditate - To focus one's mind for a period of time, in silence or with the aid of chanting.

Medium - A person who can be in contact with the spirits of the dead and who are able to communicate between the dead and the living.

Mind Control - The ability to control or influence someone's actions.

Mind Reader - A person who can supposedly discern what another person is thinking.

Miracle - An extraordinary and welcome event that is not explicable by natural or scientific laws.

Mojos - A magic charm, talisman, or spell.

Mystic - A person who seeks by contemplation and self-surrender to obtain unity with a Deity and believes in spiritual apprehension of truths that are beyond the intellect.

Nymph - A mythological spirit of nature, with the appearance of a beautiful maiden, who mainly inhabits rivers and woods.

Oracle - Someone who can act as a medium through whom advice or prophecy can be sought from the Gods.

Palmistry - The art of the practice of interpreting a person's character or predicting their future by examining the palm of their hand.

Poppet - A small figure of a human being used in witchcraft.

Possession - The state of being controlled by a demon or spirit.

Potion - A liquid with healing, magical or poisonous properties.

Prophecy - A prediction of what will happen in the future.

Psyche - The human soul, mind or spirit.

Purify - Remove contaminants from.

- GLOSSARY -

Pyrokinesis - The ability to set things on fire through the concentration of psychic power.

Quest - A long or arduous expedition to accomplish a prescribed task.

Realm - An area of knowledge or activity.

Regeneration - The action of developing or improving something.

Ritual - A ceremony consisting of a series of actions performed according to a prescribed order.

Rune - A symbol with magical significance.

Sage - A profoundly wise being

Sanctify - The remove sin and purify.

Scry - Foretell the future using a reflective object.

Shakti - External spiritual energy that is the source of all life energy.

Sigils - An inscribed symbol with magical powers.

Spell - A form of words used for magic.

Spirit - A non-physical part of a person, also knows as their soul.

Succulent - A plant such as a sedum or cactus.

Summoning - The process by which a magic-user calls forth a creature to do their bidding.

Talisman - An object, typically inscribed, that has magic powers.

Tarot - Cards, traditionally a pack of 78 with five suits, used for fortune telling.

Telekinesis - The supposed ability to move objects at a distance by mental power or non-physical means.

Telepathy - The communication of thoughts or ideas by means other than the known senses.

Tinctures - A solution of alcohol or alcohol-water and some sort of animal, vegetable or drug.

Trinket - A small ornament or item of little financial value.

- GLOSSARY -

True Owl - A typical owl and one of the two generally accepted families of owls, the other being the barn owl.

Underworld - The abode of the dead, imagined as being under the Earth.

Vampire - A nocturnal dead being that drinks blood.

Vedic - Is the period in the history of India during which the Vedas, the oldest sacred texts of Hinduism, were being composed.

Voodoo - Practised in the Caribbean and the southern US, combining elements of Roman Catholic ritual with traditional African magical and religious rites, and characterized by sorcery and spirit possession.

Werewolf - A person who changes for periods of time into a wolf, typically when there is a full moon.

Witches' Sabbaths - A midnight meeting held by witches.

Yoga - A Hindu spiritual and ascetic discipline, a part of which, including breath control, simple meditation, and the adoption of specific bodily postures, practised for health and relaxation.

Zodiac - A belt of the heavens within about 8 degrees either side of the ecliptic, including all apparent positions of the sun, moon, and most familiar planets. It is divided into twelve equal divisions or signs.

ARTIST - ILLUSTRATOR - AUTHOR
www.nonaGallery.com

@nonaGalleryArt